Fact Finders™

Biographies

Gloria Estefan

Singing Sensation

by Tim O'Shei

Consultant:
Richard Slatta
Professor of History
North Carolina State University
Raleigh, North Carolina

Capstone press

Mankato, Minnesota

Fact Finders is published by Capstone Press,
151 Good Counsel Drive, P.O. Box 669, Mankato, Minnesota 56002.
www.capstonepress.com

Library of Congress Cataloging-in-Publication Data
O'Shei, Tim.
    Gloria Estefan : singing sensation / by Tim O'Shei.
    p. cm.—(Fact finders. Biographies. Great Hispanics)
    Includes bibliographic references and index.
    ISBN-13: 978-0-7368-5439-9 (hardcover)
    ISBN-10: 0-7368-5439-8 (hardcover)
    1. Estefan, Gloria—Juvenile literature. 2. Singers—United States—Biography—Juvenile
literature. I. Title. II. Series.
ML3930.E85O84 2006
782.42164'092—dc22   2005022581

Summary: An introduction to the life of Gloria Estefan, the Cuban-born entertainer whose
    musical career has spanned decades.

Editorial Credits
Megan Schoeneberger, editor; Juliette Peters, set designer; Linda Clavel and Scott Thoms,
    book designers; Wanda Winch, photo researcher/photo editor

Photo Credits
AP Photo, 16; Chris O'Meara, 23
Corbis/Bettmann, 21
Getty Images Inc./Jamie Squire, 25
Globe Photo Inc./Kathryn Indiek, 27
Photo courtesy of Estefan Enterprises, Inc., 1, 5, 7, 8, 9, 10, 11, 13, 14, 15, 19 (all), 26
Zuma KPA/Dan Herrick - KPA, cover

1 2 3 4 5 6 11 10 09 08 07 06

Table of Contents

Chapter 1

Back on Her Feet

Gloria Estefan stood on stage, feeling stronger than ever. Music pulsed around her as she sang and danced. The crowd's cheers echoed like thunder.

On a snowy March day in 1990, Gloria's life had changed forever. A large truck rammed her tour bus. Gloria's back was broken. Doctors, friends, and fans wondered if she would ever walk again.

But Gloria didn't give up. She had her heart set on performing again. For the next year, Gloria worked hard to get healthy and strong.

Now, less than one year later, Gloria was back on her feet. But she wasn't just walking again. She was dancing.

Gloria's husband hugged her during her first concert after the tour bus accident.

Chapter 2

Growing Up

On September 1, 1957, a baby girl was born in Havana, Cuba. Her parents, José and Gloria Fajardo, named her Gloria María. They called her "Glorita," which is Spanish for "little Gloria."

Gloria's father worked for the Cuban president, Fulgencio Batista, as a bodyguard. Gloria's mother was a teacher.

FACT!

Gloria's love of music came from listening to records and the radio with her mother and grandmother.

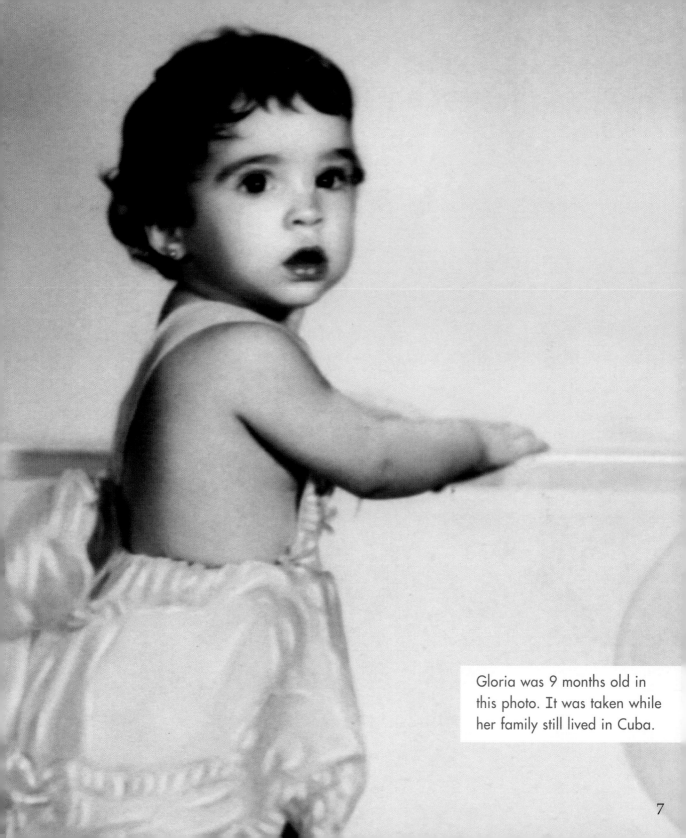

Gloria was 9 months old in this photo. It was taken while her family still lived in Cuba.

Going to Miami

When Gloria was a baby, a young **rebel** named Fidel Castro took control of the Cuban government. Castro and his supporters did not trust people like Gloria's father who had worked for Batista.

The family was not safe in Cuba. Gloria's parents decided to leave Cuba when she was 14 months old. The family flew on an airplane to Miami, Florida. They lived in a poor neighborhood where everyone spoke Spanish.

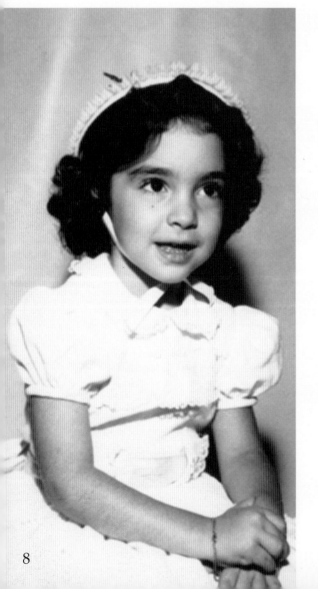

◀ This portrait shows Gloria as a young girl.

In 1961, Gloria's father returned to Cuba with a large group of fighters who wanted to overthrow Castro. The plan didn't work, and the fighters were caught. Gloria's father spent more than a year in a Cuban jail.

Gloria (center, back) and her family lived in Miami, Florida, after they left Cuba. ▼

▲ Gloria performed with her first guitar when she was 10 years old.

When Gloria's father returned to Florida, he joined the U.S. Army. In 1963, the family moved to Texas. Gloria's younger sister, Rebecca, was born there. Gloria's father went to fight in Vietnam in 1966.

Meanwhile, Gloria entered first grade and learned to speak English. For her ninth birthday, Gloria received a guitar. She enjoyed playing songs, listening to records, and singing.

Back to Miami

Gloria's father returned from Vietnam in 1968. The family moved back to Miami. However, something was wrong with Gloria's father. He had trouble walking and stumbled often. Doctors told Gloria's father that he had **multiple sclerosis**, or MS. As time passed, his illness worsened. He could not walk at all. He needed help feeding and cleaning himself. While her mother worked, Gloria spent much of her time caring for both her father and Rebecca.

⬆ Gloria's father was in the U.S. Army and served in Vietnam.

QUOTE

"When my father was ill, music was my escape. I would lock myself up in my room for hours and just sing. I wouldn't cry—I refused to cry."
—Gloria Estefan

Chapter 3

Joining a Band

Gloria was shy, but she loved singing with her friends. In the spring of 1975, as Gloria and her friends practiced to sing at a birthday party, a young man stopped to listen. He was Emilio Estefan, leader of a band called the Miami Latin Boys. He liked Gloria's voice.

Joining a Band

Soon after Gloria graduated from high school in 1975, she and her mom went to a family friend's wedding. The Miami Latin Boys were playing.

Gloria was shy about performing in front of people.

Emilio asked Gloria to sing some songs with his band. She did so well that Emilio convinced her to join the band. Since the band was no longer all male, he renamed it the Miami Sound Machine.

▲ Emilio Estefan (second from left) asked Gloria to join his band.

Over the next three years, Gloria studied **psychology** at the University of Miami. On weekends, she performed with the band. Emilio and Gloria also started dating.

A Busy Year

Gloria was busy in 1978. She graduated with a degree in psychology. But she decided to continue performing instead of looking for a psychology job. That same year, the Miami Sound Machine released its first album. On September 2, 1978, Gloria and Emilio got married.

◄ Emilio and Gloria were married the day after her 21st birthday.

Chapter 4

Singing the Hits

In the late 1970s and early 1980s, the Miami Sound Machine was very popular in Latin American countries like Panama, Peru, and Venezuela. But few people in the United States knew of the band.

Dance Music

In 1984, a song called "Dr. Beat" changed that. It was written by the Sound Machine's drummer, Kiki Garcia. The song had English lyrics instead of Spanish lyrics. "Dr. Beat" became popular in Miami, then in Europe. One year later, the band released another English song, "Conga." This song sold 2 million copies all over the world.

The Miami Sound Machine became known for their high-energy performances.

Throughout the 1980s, Gloria and the band recorded many songs. In 1988, they scored their first number one hit, "Anything for You." Other songs included "Words Get in the Way" and "Rhythm Is Gonna Getcha."

As the band's music became more popular, the group became known as Gloria Estefan & the Miami Sound Machine. Putting Gloria's name first showed how important she was to the band. One by one, the other members left. New musicians replaced them. But Gloria remained.

Still Shy

Gloria still considered herself a shy person. Early in her career, she felt nervous on stage but knew she had to put on a dazzling show for her fans. Gloria watched videos of her performances, looking for ways to improve her act.

The Miami Sound Machine released many albums in the 1970s and 1980s.

Chapter 5

Showing Strength

Gloria's fame helped her make political statements. In 1987, the band was invited to play at the closing ceremonies of the Pan American Games in Indianapolis, Indiana. The Cuban team was angry. They didn't want to listen to a group of musicians who had fled their country. But Gloria insisted on playing so that the band could show the Cubans what freedom really means.

Gloria also spoke out against drug abuse. Her statements impressed President George H. W. Bush. In 1990, Bush invited Gloria, Emilio, and their son, Nayib, to the White House.

Gloria and her husband met President George H. W. Bush in 1990.

Terrible Accident

On a snowy day in March 1990, Gloria was traveling on her tour bus from New York City to Syracuse, New York. Gloria was resting on a couch when a semitruck hit the bus from behind. The impact threw Gloria off the couch.

Gloria was rushed to the nearest hospital, where doctors learned that she had broken her back. No one was sure if Gloria would ever walk again.

Impressive Recovery

Doctors fixed Gloria's back in surgery the next day. They inserted two 8-inch (20-centimeter) metal braces. Gloria spent the next several months at home. She had to practice walking and getting dressed.

Gloria wrote a song about her recovery called "Coming out of the Dark." One year after the accident, she went on a 29-country world tour. The first concert was in Miami. She opened the concert by singing "Get on Your Feet."

Gloria's son (right) gave her flowers when she returned home after her accident. ➡

Chapter 6

A Role Model

Gloria kept recording popular songs in the 1990s. One of the most memorable songs was "Reach." Gloria wrote the song with her friend Diane Warren and performed it during the 1996 Summer Olympics in Atlanta, Georgia.

Gloria also helped many charities. In 1992, she and Emilio hosted a benefit concert to raise money for **victims** of Hurricane Andrew in south Florida. In 1997, she started the Gloria Estefan Foundation. This group gives money to pay for educational and music programs for needy children. The foundation also supports spinal cord research.

In 1999, Gloria performed during the Super Bowl halftime show in Miami, Florida.

▲ Gloria and her children were present when Emilio received a star on the Hollywood Walk of Fame.

Moving On

In 2004, Gloria stopped touring. She stays close to home. She writes songs and spends time with her family, which now includes her daughter, Emily. Emilio runs their music and restaurant company, Estefan Enterprises.

Gloria has faced difficulties in her life. She has overcome shyness and a painful injury. With hard work, Gloria has shown that anyone can achieve his or her dreams.

Fast Facts

Full name: Gloria María Fajardo Estefan

Birth: September 1, 1957

Birthplace: Havana, Cuba

Hometown: Miami, Florida

Parents: José and Gloria Fajardo

Sister: Rebecca

Husband: Emilio

Children: Nayib, Emily

Education:
> Bachelor of Science in psychology, University of Miami, 1978

Achievements:
> 24 albums recorded
> 70 million albums and singles sold worldwide
> 33 Top 10 songs

Time Line

Gloria María Fajardo is born September 1 in Havana, Cuba.

The Fajardo family escapes Cuba and moves to Miami, Florida.

Gloria enters college and joins the Miami Latin Boys; they become the Miami Sound Machine.

Gloria finishes college and marries Emilio Estefan; the Miami Sound Machine releases its first album.

1957   **1958**   **1975**   **1978**

1954   **1959**   **1964**   **1975**

The Vietnam War begins.

Fidel Castro overthrows Fulgencio Batista to become leader of Cuba.

The Vietnam War ends.

The Civil Rights Act outlaws discrimination in the United States.

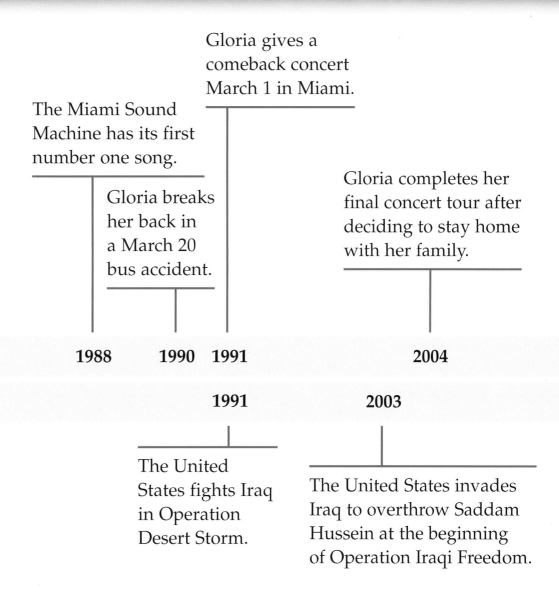

The Miami Sound
Machine has its first
number one song.

Gloria gives a
comeback concert
March 1 in Miami.

Gloria breaks
her back in
a March 20
bus accident.

Gloria completes her
final concert tour after
deciding to stay home
with her family.

1988 **1990** **1991** **2004**

1991 **2003**

The United
States fights Iraq
in Operation
Desert Storm.

The United States invades
Iraq to overthrow Saddam
Hussein at the beginning
of Operation Iraqi Freedom.

Glossary

multiple sclerosis (MUHL-tuh-puhl skluh-ROH-suhss)—a serious disease in which small areas of the brain and spinal cord are destroyed; multiple sclerosis can cause paralysis and muscle tremors.

psychology (sye-KOH-luh-jee)—the study of the mind, emotions, and human behavior

rebel (REB-uhl)—someone who fights against a government or against the people in charge of something

victim (VIK-tuhm)—a person who is hurt, killed, or made to suffer

Internet Sites

FactHound offers a safe, fun way to find Internet sites related to this book. All of the sites on FactHound have been researched by our staff.

Here's how:

1. Visit *www.facthound.com*
2. Type in this special code **0736854398** for age-appropriate sites. Or enter a search word related to this book for a more general search.
3. Click on the **Fetch It** button.

FactHound will fetch the best sites for you!

Read More

Kramer, Barbara. *Gloria Estefan: Never Give Up*. Awesome Values in Famous Lives. Berkeley Heights, N.J.: Enslow Elementary, 2005.

Lee, Sally. *Gloria Estefan: Superstar of Song.* Latino Biography Library. Berkeley Heights, N.J.: Enslow, 2005.

Phillips, Jane. *Gloria Estefan.* Women of Achievement. Broomall, Penn.: Chelsea House, 2001.

Index